Project

Ancient Egypt

Simon Adams

Miles Kelly

First published in 2013 by Miles Kelly Publishing Ltd
Harding's Barn, Bardfield End Green, Thaxted, Essex, CM6 3PX, UK

Copyright © Miles Kelly Publishing Ltd 2013

This edition printed 2018

2 4 6 8 10 9 7 5 3 1

Publishing Director Belinda Gallagher
Creative Director Jo Cowan
Senior Editor Claire Philip
Designers Andrea Slane, Joe Jones
Consultant Rupert Matthews
Indexer Jane Parker
Image Manager Liberty Newton
Production Elizabeth Collins, Caroline Kelly
Reprographics Stephan Davis, Thom Allaway
Assets Lorraine King

ISBN 978-1-78617-526-7

Printed in China

British Library Cataloguing-in-Publication Data
A catalogue record for this book is available from the British Library

Made with paper from a sustainable forest

www.mileskelly.net

IMPORTANT NOTICE
The publisher and author cannot be held responsible for any injuries, damage or loss resulting from the use or misuse of any of the information in this book.

SAFETY FIRST!
Be careful when using glue or anything sharp, such as scissors. Always ask an adult if there is a note to ask for help.

WARNING!
One project contains nuts: anyone with a known nut allergy must use the alternative ingredients suggested. We advise caution with this recipe.

If your project doesn't work the first time, try again — just have fun!

How to use the projects

This book is packed full of amazing facts about ancient Egypt. There are also 11 cool projects, designed to make the subject come alive.

Before you start a project:

• Read the instructions carefully and ask an adult if you need help.

• Gather all the supplies you need.

• Clear a surface to work on and cover it with newspaper.

• Wear an apron or old t-shirt to protect your clothing.

Notes for helpers:

• Children will need supervision for the projects, usually because they require the use of scissors, or preparation beforehand.

• Read the instructions together before starting and help to gather the equipment.

Supplies
The equipment should be easy to find, around the house or from a craft store. Always ask before using materials from home.

Numbered stages
Each stage of the project is numbered and the illustrations will help you. Follow the stages in the order shown to complete the project. If glue or paint is used, make sure it is dry before moving onto the next stage.

Shabti servant

Don't want to do any work in the underworld? Then make a shabti to do it for you!

SUPPLIES

newspaper to cover your work surface and for the model • masking tape • plaster of Paris bandages cut into 2.5 cm wide strips • felt tip pens • small bowl of water

HOW TO MAKE

1. Scrunch the newspaper into an oblong shape. One end should be flat so that the shabti stands up. The other end (the head) should be rounded. Wrap completely with masking tape.

2. Dip the plaster of Paris strips in the water and then wrap around the shabti, smoothing it down with your fingers as you go.

3. Leave to dry, then draw a face on the head end. Then decorate the body using the felt tip pens.

4. Lastly, under the face, write down a job you would like your shabti to do.

TIDY MY ROOM

❶ ❷ ❸

CONTENTS

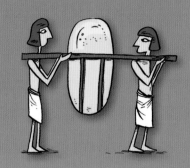

LIFE-GIVING RIVER

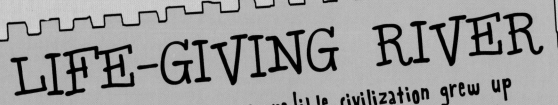

Around 5000 years ago an incredible civilization grew up along the banks of the River Nile in Egypt. The ancient Egyptians were very advanced for their time, building vast towns, beautiful temples and an impressive empire.

▼ The Egyptians made full use of the River Nile for their every need.

Pyramids

Farmers cutting corn

Traders selling goods

A MIGHTY RIVER

The River Nile rises in Central Africa and flows 6650 km northwards, through Egypt, on its journey to the Mediterranean Sea. This impressive waterway allowed the Egyptians to flourish — it was their main form of transport, carrying boats laden with animals and goods to trade.

Nile Delta

Lower Egypt

AFRICA

Upper Egypt

River Nile

▶ Most Egyptian settlements grew up along the river, which provided water to an otherwise dry land.

MUD, GLORIOUS MUD!

Every June the River Nile flooded, bursting its banks and covering the land with a dark soil called silt. Farmers planted crops in this thick silt. The event was hugely important to the Egyptians, as it meant they could grow plenty of food. They recorded the rising water levels with a nilometer.

Egypt through time

Predynastic Period 5500–3100 BC	Early Dynasties 3100–2010 BC	Middle Kingdom 2010–1539 BC	New Kingdom 1539–664 BC	Late Period 664–30 BC

5000 BC Civilization begins to flourish alongside the Nile

3000 BC Upper and Lower Egypt are united

2600 BC Pyramids are built at Giza

Trade, art and literature prosper in Egypt

1500 BC Egyptian empire extends into the Middle East

30 BC Egypt becomes part of the Roman Empire

Oxen pulling ploughs

Papyrus reeds

Farmer using a shaduf

Trade boat

Reed boat used for hunting and fishing

Hippos

Float your boat

The Egyptians built simple boats from papyrus reeds, which grew on the riverbanks. Make your own with drinking straws!

SUPPLIES

20 drinking straws with flexible ends (try and use all the same colour) • sticky tape scissors

HOW TO MAKE

1. Carefully snip up the ends of two straws, then slide them together so they are joined. Make sure the bendy parts of the straws are at either end.

2. Repeat this process with the other straws so that you have ten in total. Make sure they are the same length by pushing them together in equal amounts.

3. Lay the ten straws next to each other and wrap sticky tape firmly around the middle. Bend the straws at the flexible necks.

4. Stick tape around the bendy ends of the straws to secure them in place. Now you are ready to float your boat!

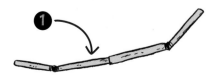

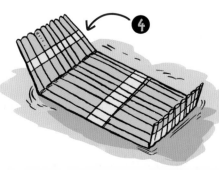

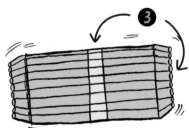

ALMIGHTY RULERS

A long line of kings — and some queens — known as pharaohs, ruled ancient Egypt. The pharaoh was the most important person in the land. His role was to hand out justice, ensure law and order and protect Egypt from foreign invaders.

▶ Rameses II was one of Egypt's greatest warrior pharaohs, and became known as Rameses the Great.

WHEELS OF WAR

The pharaohs fought their enemies with vast armies that rode on two-wheeled chariots. Around 1275 BC, Rameses II fought the battle of Kadesh against the Hittites (in what is now Turkey) for control of Syria and Lebanon. The Egyptians won the brutal battle.

Charioteers steered during battle

Arrows were shot at the enemy

A LIVING GOD

Families of pharaohs (dynasties) ruled Egypt over its long history. Each pharaoh had a string of names and titles that linked him to the gods. The pharaoh was the head of religion and high priest of every temple. When he died, it was believed his spirit joined the gods.

A pharaoh's headdress

Ask an adult for help!

When pharaohs weren't wearing a crown they wore a simple headdress, called a nemes. Make your own and be a king for a day!

SUPPLIES

a long piece of striped fabric that will cover your hair (or paint an old pillowcase)
A3 yellow card • 4 safety pins
15 cm square white card
colouring pencils • glue
scissors • measuring tape

HOW TO MAKE

1. First, make a card headband by measuring the circumference of your head, then cutting a strip of yellow card to the same length. Stick either end together with glue.

2. Draw a cobra head onto the white card, add a scale pattern, tongue, fangs and eyes, and colour it in. Cut it out carefully with the scissors.

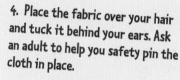

3. Glue the cobra to the centre of the headband.

4. Place the fabric over your hair and tuck it behind your ears. Ask an adult to help you safety pin the cloth in place.

5. Place the headband over your head to hold the headdress in place.

Two horses pulled each war chariot

COOL QUEEN

Just occasionally, a woman held the throne of Egypt. One of the most well known and successful is Hatshepsut. She ruled Egypt on behalf of her young son, but soon took power herself. She said her father was Amun, the king of the gods, and ruled the country for over 20 years. Vast trading expeditions were sent north to Lebanon and south to Punt in Africa in search of precious goods during her reign.

Know your place!

There were levels of importance in Egyptian society.

1. Pharaohs

2. Viziers (powerful officials)

3. Priests

4. Scribes and nobles

5. Skilled craftsmen

6. Unskilled workers

LAND OF THE GODS

Hundreds of different gods were worshipped in ancient Egypt. Some had specific roles, such as helping the crops to grow or the Nile to flood. Gods could be both cruel and kind, and went in and out of fashion. Over the years the names, role and appearances of some gods changed.

▼ Some gods were worshipped across Egypt, while each of the 42 districts had its own local god. Here are some of the most important gods of all.

Horus – god of the sky

Hathor – goddess of love, music and dance

Osiris – god of the dead

Amun-Ra – king of all gods

Sobek – god of the Nile

Ma'at – goddess of truth

Who was top god?
? ? ? ? ?

Ankh amulet

The ankh was a popular amulet shaped like the hieroglyphic sign for the word 'life'. Make one and see if it brings you luck!

SUPPLIES

10 tbsp fine sawdust • 20 tbsp flour • water bowl • sandpaper • gold paint • spoon • old plate newspaper (to cover work surface) • string

HOW TO MAKE

1. Mix the sawdust and flour together in the bowl using a spoon. Slowly add enough water to turn the mixture into soft dough.

2. Take some of the dough, place it on the plate and mould it into an ankh shape.

3. Place the ankh in sunlight or near a radiator to dry – it may take a few days.

4. Once dry, rub away the rough edges with sandpaper and paint the ankh gold.

5. When the paint is dry, loop a piece of string through the hole and either hang the ankh up or wear it as a necklace!

LUCKY CHARMS

The Egyptians wore amulets to bring them luck and protect them from danger. They often took the form of gods or sacred animals. The wedjat eye amulet represented the eye of the god Horus, who looked like a falcon.

Ankh

Wedjat eye

▶ The cat goddess Bastet was a symbol of motherhood.

Bes – god of the home

Isis – goddess of magic

HERE KITTY, KITTY!

Animals were often used to represent different gods. The cat goddess Bastet protected the pharaohs. At first she was shown with the head of a lioness but later she was shown as a pet cat.

9

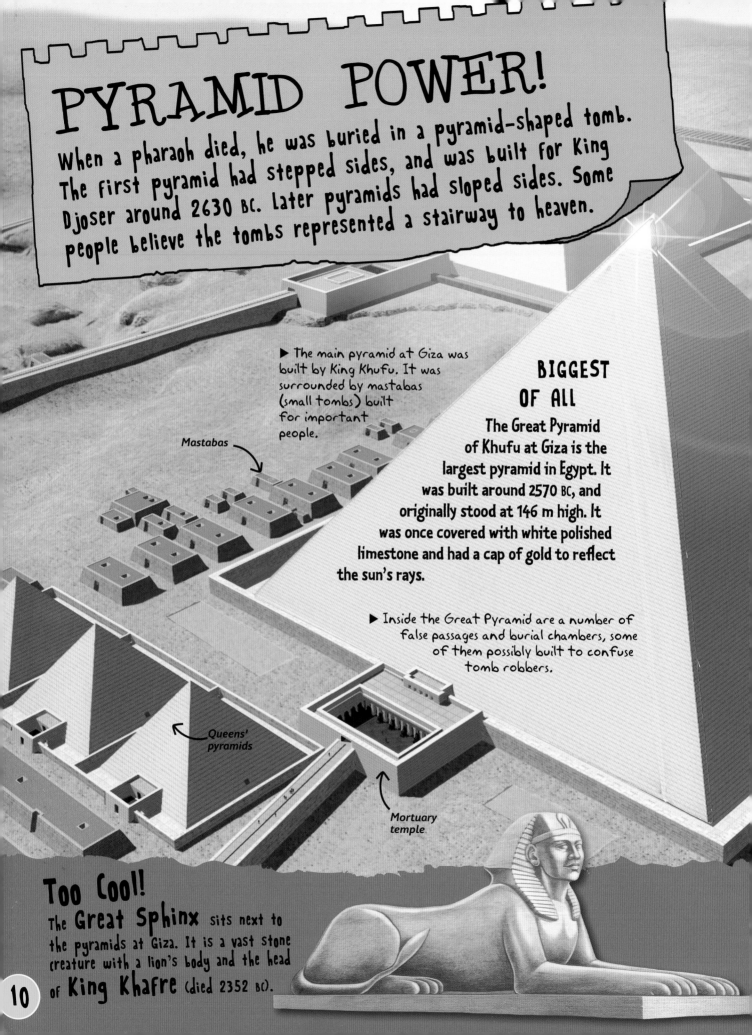

PYRAMID POWER!

When a pharaoh died, he was buried in a pyramid-shaped tomb. The first pyramid had stepped sides, and was built for King Djoser around 2630 BC. Later pyramids had sloped sides. Some people believe the tombs represented a stairway to heaven.

▶ The main pyramid at Giza was built by King Khufu. It was surrounded by mastabas (small tombs) built for important people.

Mastabas

BIGGEST OF ALL

The Great Pyramid of Khufu at Giza is the largest pyramid in Egypt. It was built around 2570 BC, and originally stood at 146 m high. It was once covered with white polished limestone and had a cap of gold to reflect the sun's rays.

▶ Inside the Great Pyramid are a number of false passages and burial chambers, some of them possibly built to confuse tomb robbers.

Queens' pyramids

Mortuary temple

Too Cool!
The **Great Sphinx** sits next to the pyramids at Giza. It is a vast stone creature with a lion's body and the head of **King Khafre** (died 2352 BC).

FULL OF TREASURE!

The pyramids were often robbed, so from 1482 BC onwards pharaohs were buried in secret tombs hidden away in a remote valley in the south of Egypt. This area was known as the Valley of the Kings. Great efforts were made to conceal the entrances to the tombs, which consisted of long passages leading down into the main burial chamber.

WoW

Western cemetery

BLOCK BY BLOCK

More than 2,300,000 limestone blocks were used to build the Great Pyramid. Incredibly, every block weighed 2.5 tonnes. We still do not know exactly how the Egyptians managed to lift such massive blocks into place. The 100,000 or so workers would have had to place 12 blocks into position every hour of every day and night for 20 years to complete the pyramid!

▶ Building the pyramids was an exhausting task undertaken by many workers, who lived near the site. Amazingly, more than 80 pyramids were built in ancient Egypt.

Pyramid model

It took thousands of workers many years to build a pyramid. You can make your own in a few minutes!

SUPPLIES

A2 sheet of yellow card ● long ruler pencil ● scissors ● PVA glue

HOW TO MAKE

1. Measure and mark out a 20 x 20 cm square on the card.

2. On each side of the square, mark the middle point at 10 cm.

3. From this point, measure a 15-cm line at a right angle, then draw a line from each corner of the square to form a triangle. Do the same on the other sides.

4. Add tabs (as shown below), then using the scissors, carefully score all of the fold lines before cutting out the pyramid.

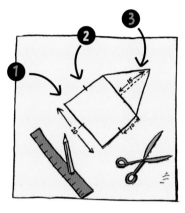

5. Put some glue on the underside of each tab, then fold up the four sides one at a time. Press the tabs firmly to secure them in place.

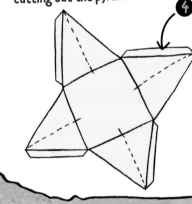

MAGNIFICENT TEMPLES

The Egyptians built grand stone temples for their many gods to live in. They believed that the god's spirit lived in a statue, which was housed in a small inner sanctuary. Regular festivals attracted large crowds, but only priests and the pharaoh could enter this space.

SACRED PLACES

Most Egyptian temples followed a similar layout. They had a high outer wall with a large entrance gate. This led to a courtyard where ordinary worshippers met and prayed. Beyond this was the dark hall, filled with tall columns. At the far end lay the inner sanctuary — the holiest place of all, where a statue of the god was housed.

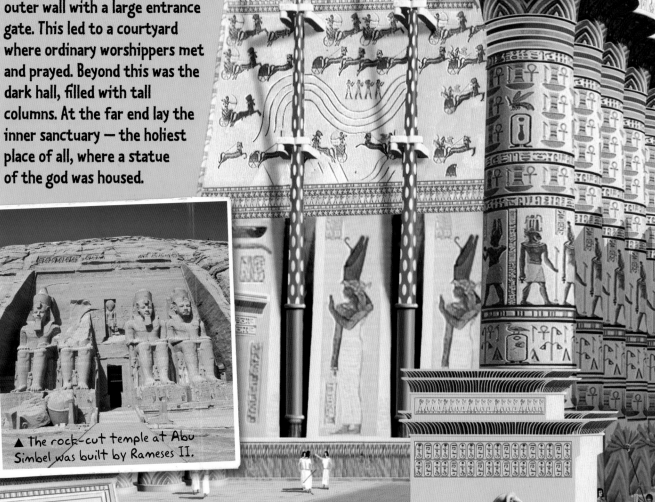

▲ The rock-cut temple at Abu Simbel was built by Rameses II.

Every day, temple priests brought new clothes, food and **even make-up** to the statue of the god.

ONLY ONE GOD?

When Akhenaten became pharaoh in 1353 BC, he ordered his subjects to stop worshipping multiple gods. Instead they had to worship Aten, the Lord of Heaven and Earth. He closed down all other temples, but they were reopened after his death. Akhenaten was struck off the official list of pharaohs.

▶ Akhenaten was represented by a sun disc, the symbol of the god Aten.

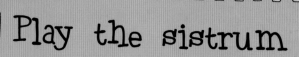

▼ Amun Ra's temple at Karnak was once an important place of worship.

POINT TO THE SUN

Outside most temples stood a tall, slender obelisk. An obelisk is a stone pillar with four sloping sides topped by a little pyramid, sometimes covered with gold to reflect the sun.

▶ Obelisks were cut from a single piece of stone. They were carved with the names of pharaohs.

Play the sistrum

Noblewomen sometimes acted as priestesses at festivals. They played music on rattle-like instruments called sistrums. Now you can too!

SUPPLIES

wire clothes hanger • 3 x 30 cm lengths of jewellery wire
at least 36 brass paper fasteners (or buttons)
electrical or masking tape • kitchen roll

HOW TO MAKE

1. Ask an adult to help you pull the bottom of the hanger so that it becomes a long U shape. Carefully squeeze the hook closed to make a circular handle. If there are any sharp points wrap them in kitchen roll and then cover with tape.

2. Take a piece of jewellery wire and tie one end of it to the hanger, halfway up the U shape. If it comes loose, use some tape to secure.

3. Bend at least twelve brass fasteners around the wire, then attach the other end to the other side of the hanger.

4. Do the same to the second and third piece of wire, one 2.5 cm above the first wire and one 2.5 cm below it. Then shake the sistrum to make a joyful noise!

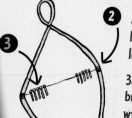

BURYING THE DEAD

When they died, the pharaohs were buried in style! Once they were mummified, (see inside) their bodies were placed inside a series of coffins, each fitting snugly inside another. This set was then placed inside a large outer coffin known as a sarcophagus.

▶ Tutankhamun is one of the most famous pharaohs, and his grand tomb shows how extravagant ancient Egyptian burials could be. This exploded view shows the layers of coffins in which he was buried.

Inner coffin cover

Gold face mask

Wrapped mummy

Inner gold coffin

Middle wooden coffin

Outer wooden coffin

1

Tutankhamun's burial chamber was filled almost entirely by four wooden shrines, each one highly decorated and fitting snugly inside each other (not shown here).

2

Inside the four wooden shrines was a stone sarcophagus. Its outside was carved with pictures of gods. Inside were three coffins fitting inside each other. The outer two were made of wood.

3

The inner coffin was made of solid gold. The gold coffin was shaped to fit Tutankhamun's body, and weighed 110.4 kg.

4

Inside the gold coffin was the mummified body of Tutankhamun. The head and shoulders were covered with a gold mask that had a portrait of the pharaoh's face.

Middle
coffin cover

Outer coffin
cover

Too Cool!

Human-shaped coffins were popular from the 1700s BC.

Some **coffins had maps** on them to help the deceased find their way in the afterlife.

Coffins were made of **cedar** or other wood, others of **basketwork** or layers of **linen**, strengthened with plaster. Some were even made from **solid gold!**

▶ Tutankhamun's tomb was rediscovered by Howard Carter in 1922 with its contents still largely intact.

THE YOUNG KING

Tutankhamun died in 1322 BC and was buried in the Valley of the Kings. His burial chamber lay behind three sealed doors at the rear of his underground tomb. The tomb was also filled with furniture, jewels, weapons, musical instruments and other items the pharaoh would need in the afterlife.

LIFE AFTER DEATH

Egyptians believed that when they died, their soul would travel to the underworld. They called this world Duat, and it was a place of many terrors to be overcome. If the soul survived, it would enter a heavenly afterlife ruled over by the god Osiris.

Anubis

▶This illustration comes from the Book of the Dead of Hunefer, a scribe that lived around 1300 BC.

Hunefer's soul

The Devourer

4 If Hunefer lied, and his heart was heavier than the feather, the goddess known as the Devourer of the Dead would eat his heart.

2 Anubis leads the dead man's soul into the Hall of Two Truths. Here the heart of the dead man is placed on a set of scales opposite the feather of truth.

3 Forty-two gods question Hunefer's soul. If it tells the truth and its heart is lighter than the feather, Thoth will let him go to the Kingdom of Osiris.

1 A long scroll of papyrus, known as The Book of the Dead, was buried with the mummy. It contained spells, which if recited properly would help the soul pass through Duat.

SERVANT STATUES

There were still lots of jobs, such as farming, to do in the afterlife. Not everyone wanted to do manual labour for Osiris so Egyptians were often buried with little figures of workers called shabtis. They believed they would leap to life and work in the fields in their place.

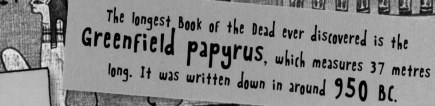

The longest Book of the Dead ever discovered is the **Greenfield papyrus**, which measures 37 metres long. It was written down in around **950 BC.**

5

Luckily the dead man's heart is lighter than the feather, so he gets to travel on. The falcon-headed god, Horus, leads him to Osiris.

Thoth

Horus

JUST LIKE HEAVEN

If the dead man's soul successfully passes through the hall of judgement it gets to enter the field of reeds, a heavenly place very much like the Nile delta. Here, in the land of the god Osiris, the soul lived in eternal happiness.

▲ This wall painting is from the tomb of Sennedjem at Luxor. It shows Sennedjem and his wife planting and harvesting in Egyptian paradise.

Shabti servant

Don't want to do any work in the underworld? Then make a shabti to do it for you!

SUPPLIES

newspaper to cover your work surface and for the model • masking tape • plaster of Paris bandages cut into 2.5 cm wide strips • felt tip pens • small bowl of water

HOW TO MAKE

1. Scrunch the newspaper into an oblong shape. One end should be flat so that the shabti stands up. The other end (the head) should be rounded. Wrap completely with masking tape.

2. Dip the plaster of Paris strips in the water and then wrap around the shabti, smoothing it down with your fingers as you go.

3. Leave to dry, then draw a face on the head end. Then decorate the body using the felt tip pens.

4. Lastly, under the face, write down a job you would like your shabti to do.

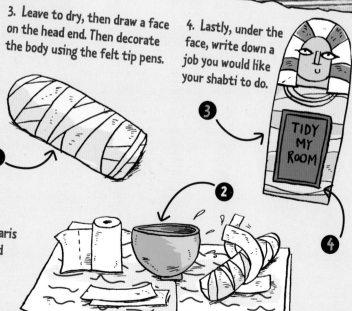

TIDY MY ROOM

1

2

3

4

WRITING IT DOWN

The Egyptian alphabet was made up of around 700 pictures called hieroglyphs. Each picture represented a sound, object or idea. This complicated system was developed in around 3100 BC, and is one of the oldest written languages in the world.

Spare writing tool

◄ This engraving shows a scribe called Mery writing hieroglyphics.

Hieroglyphic symbol for 'M'

Hieroglyphic symbol for 'F'

Hieroglyphs can be read from **left to right**, or **right to left**... or **top to bottom!**

OFFICIAL WRITERS
Scribes were some of the most important people in Egypt, as only they could write hieroglyphs. They began training at the age of nine and studied for five years. Once qualified, they wrote official documents on scrolls of papyrus and advised stonemasons on how to carve the script in temples and other buildings.

◄ This ancient Egyptian legal document is written in hieratic script.

THREE DIFFERENT SCRIPTS

Hieroglyphics were kept deliberately complex so that only trained scribes could write them. They were used for temples, tombs, monuments and religious documents. A faster-written version, known as hieratic script, was used for legal and business documents. Around 800 BC, the even faster demotic script was developed.

Hieroglyphic challenge

Use this chart to write your name in pictures, just like the Egyptians did!

SUPPLIES

colouring pencils • paper • scissors

HOW TO MAKE

1. Looking at the chart, copy the hieroglyphs that make up the letters of your name. You could use a different colour for each symbol.

2. Draw a border around your name and colour it in. Once cut out, you could use it as a sign for your bedroom door.

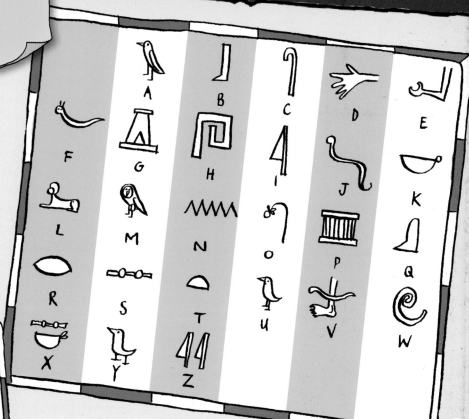

DAILY LIFE

Most Egyptians lived in houses with four small rooms in which to live, eat and sleep. The wealthy lived along the Nile in sparkling-white villas with many rooms, including guest bedrooms, servant's quarters and even indoor bathrooms!

1

BAKING BREAD
Bread was an important part of every meal. Loaves came in all shapes and sizes and were cooked on a hot oven. The poor ate coarse brown bread while richer people enjoyed white bread.

2

FEELING THIRSTY
Beer was the most popular drink, and was stored in large pottery jars. Spices and dates were added to improve its taste. It had to be drunk quite quickly before it went sour.

▶ This house has two floors and a large courtyard at the front in which daily tasks were carried out.

3

MAKING CLOTHES
Clothes were made of linen woven on a loom from the fibres of the flax plant. The finer the clothing the wealthier the wearer.

4. REED CANOPY
A simple canopy of reeds laid over a frame kept the intense sunshine off the roof, and provided some much-needed shade.

5. FLAT ROOF TOPS
Houses had flat roofs. People spent a lot of time working and playing on them, and even slept there during hot summer months.

6. MAKING BRICKS
Bricks were made of mud strengthened with straw and pebbles. The bricks were made in wooden frames and then left out in the sun to dry and harden.

7. POTTERY SKILLS
Simple pots and plates were made of clay and fired in a hot kiln. The pots were used for cooking and storing food and drink. Plates were used to serve food.

Egyptian sweets

This dessert was served at a feast or family celebration. Why not make some for a party?

SUPPLIES
12 pitted dates • walnut pieces (or puffed rice cereal)
125 ml runny honey • 1 tsp ground cinnamon • 2 bowls
400 g ground almonds (or desiccated coconut)

HOW TO MAKE

1. Pour the honey into a bowl and mix in the cinnamon.

2. Place the ground almonds (or desiccated coconut) into another bowl.

3. Stuff each date with walnut pieces (or puffed rice cereal).

4. Dip each stuffed date into the honey and then roll them in the almonds (or coconut). Serve immediately!

WARNING!
If you have a nut allergy, use the alternative ingredients suggested.

25

A CHILD IN EGYPT

In ancient Egypt education was for the lucky few. The boys of rich, important parents went to school at the age of five or six to study, while poor boys learned their father's trade. Girls mostly stayed at home and learned domestic duties.

IN THE CLASSROOM

Boys started school at the age of five and learned both hieroglyphic and hieratic scripts. They mostly copied lists of words and extracts from books onto wooden boards, as papyrus, a type of paper made from reeds, was very expensive.

Teacher instructing his class

Children from rich and noble families were educated in the royal palace along with the pharaoh's children.

▼ Pupils would sit cross-legged on the floor, and put their hands up to answer a question.

Boys wore a ponytail known as the 'side-lock of youth'

A papyrus scroll is unwrapped and examined

Papyrus paper

If you want to write like an Egyptian first make your own 'papyrus' paper.

SUPPLIES
greaseproof paper • white PVA glue
large bowl • water • strips of brown
paper • paints, crayons or felt tips
old wooden spoon

HOW TO MAKE

1. Mix half of the bottle of glue with the same amount of water in the bowl, using the wooden spoon.

2. Dip one strip of paper into the glue mixture covering it completely. Take it out and slide it between your fingers to remove any excess glue. Place it flat on the greaseproof paper.

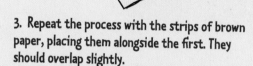

3. Repeat the process with the strips of brown paper, placing them alongside the first. They should overlap slightly.

4. Make a second and third layer of strips to go on top – placing them at alternative angles. Press each layer down to make them smooth, then leave to dry overnight.

5. Once your paper is dry, cut it out so it doesn't have a greaseproof paper border. You can write messages and decorate it.

▶ The family was the centre of Egyptian life. At its heart were the women, who ran the family and produced children.

Pupils practised writing on wooden palettes

GIRLS IN ANCIENT EGYPT
Although girls from richer families were sometimes educated, most learned skills from their mother. When they grew up, they could have a career as a courtier to the queen or they could become a priestess. Others worked as weavers, servants, musicians or dancers.

Toys and games
Egyptian children had a wide range of toys to play with, including these!

Toy cat

Toy horse

Doll

TIME TO PARTY

The ancient Egyptians didn't spend all their time building pyramids and worshipping gods — they enjoyed themselves too! They had large public festivals with singing, music and dancing, and also played games to amuse themselves.

▶ Parties in Egypt were lively events with music and dancing.

Drum

Lyre

Double oboe

Harp

Too Cool!

Many Egyptians played a game called **mehen** on a circular board that looked like a **curled-up snake.**

The Egyptians played a wide variety of **string** and **percussion instruments.** Their music probably had a **strong beat!**

Women played **instruments** and **danced** for the guests' entertainment.

GAME ON!

One of the Egyptians' favourite board games was senet. The game symbolized a struggle against the evil forces that prevented you from reaching the realm of the god Osiris.